50 Beginner Sweet Treat Recipes for Home

By: Kelly Johnson

Table of Contents

- Chocolate Chip Cookies
- Brownies
- Rice Krispie Treats
- No-Bake Cheesecake
- Banana Bread
- Cupcakes
- Peanut Butter Cookies
- Apple Crisp
- Lemon Bars
- Sugar Cookies
- Oatmeal Cookies
- Chocolate Mousse
- Mini Fruit Tarts
- Snickerdoodles
- Muffins
- Pudding Cups
- Cookie Dough Truffles
- Chocolate-Covered Pretzels
- Granola Bars
- Fruit Salad
- Cake Pops
- S'mores
- Shortbread Cookies
- Eclairs
- Fudge
- Blondies
- Chocolate Bark
- Pancakes with Syrup
- Strawberry Shortcake
- Biscotti
- Tiramisu
- Chocolate Dipped Strawberries
- Meringue Cookies
- Energy Bites
- Chocolate Lava Cake

- Crepes
- Coconut Macaroons
- Rice Pudding
- Cinnamon Rolls
- Milkshakes
- Fruit Smoothies
- Chocolate Banana Pops
- Apple Pie
- Gingerbread Cookies
- Cookie Cups
- Pumpkin Spice Muffins
- Sweet Potato Pie
- Churros
- Ice Cream Sundaes
- Pecan Pie

Chocolate Chip Cookies

Ingredients:
1 cup butter, softened
3/4 cup brown sugar
3/4 cup granulated sugar
1 tsp vanilla extract
2 large eggs
2 1/4 cups all-purpose flour
1 tsp baking soda
1/2 tsp salt
2 cups chocolate chips

Instructions:

1. Preheat oven to 350°F (175°C).
2. In a bowl, cream together butter, brown sugar, and granulated sugar. Add vanilla and eggs, mixing well.
3. In another bowl, whisk flour, baking soda, and salt. Gradually combine with wet ingredients. Fold in chocolate chips.
4. Drop spoonfuls onto a baking sheet and bake for 10-12 minutes until golden.

Brownies

Ingredients:
1/2 cup butter
1 cup sugar
2 large eggs
1 tsp vanilla extract
1/3 cup cocoa powder
1/2 cup flour
1/4 tsp salt
1/4 tsp baking powder

Instructions:

1. Preheat oven to 350°F (175°C). Grease a baking pan.
2. Melt butter, then mix in sugar, eggs, and vanilla.
3. Stir in cocoa, flour, salt, and baking powder until combined.
4. Pour into the pan and bake for 20-25 minutes. Let cool before cutting.

Rice Krispie Treats

Ingredients:
3 tbsp butter
4 cups mini marshmallows
6 cups Rice Krispies cereal

Instructions:

1. Melt butter in a large saucepan over low heat.
2. Add marshmallows and stir until melted.
3. Remove from heat and mix in Rice Krispies until well coated.
4. Press into a greased pan and let cool before cutting.

No-Bake Cheesecake

Ingredients:
1 1/2 cups graham cracker crumbs
1/4 cup sugar
1/3 cup butter, melted
8 oz cream cheese, softened
1/2 cup sugar
1 tsp vanilla extract
2 cups whipped cream

Instructions:

1. Combine crumbs, 1/4 cup sugar, and butter; press into the bottom of a springform pan.
2. In a bowl, beat cream cheese, 1/2 cup sugar, and vanilla until smooth.
3. Fold in whipped cream and spread over crust. Refrigerate for at least 4 hours before serving.

Banana Bread

Ingredients:
2-3 ripe bananas, mashed
1/3 cup melted butter
1 tsp baking soda
Pinch of salt
3/4 cup sugar
1 large egg, beaten
1 tsp vanilla extract
1 cup all-purpose flour

Instructions:

1. Preheat oven to 350°F (175°C).
2. In a bowl, mix mashed bananas with melted butter.
3. Stir in baking soda and salt. Add sugar, egg, and vanilla; mix well.
4. Finally, stir in flour until just combined. Pour into a greased loaf pan and bake for 60-65 minutes.

Cupcakes

Ingredients:
1 1/2 cups all-purpose flour
1 cup sugar
1/2 cup butter, softened
2 large eggs
1/2 cup milk
1 3/4 tsp baking powder
1 tsp vanilla extract

Instructions:

1. Preheat oven to 350°F (175°C). Line a cupcake tin with liners.
2. Cream together butter and sugar. Beat in eggs and vanilla.
3. Combine flour and baking powder; mix in alternately with milk.
4. Fill liners 2/3 full and bake for 18-20 minutes.

Peanut Butter Cookies

Ingredients:
1 cup peanut butter
1 cup sugar
1 large egg
1 tsp vanilla extract

Instructions:

1. Preheat oven to 350°F (175°C).
2. In a bowl, mix peanut butter, sugar, egg, and vanilla until smooth.
3. Roll into balls, place on a baking sheet, and flatten with a fork.
4. Bake for 10-12 minutes until set.

Apple Crisp

Ingredients:
4 cups sliced apples
1/2 cup sugar
1 tsp cinnamon
1/2 cup rolled oats
1/2 cup flour
1/2 cup brown sugar
1/4 cup butter, softened

Instructions:

1. Preheat oven to 350°F (175°C).
2. Toss apples with sugar and cinnamon; place in a greased baking dish.
3. In a bowl, mix oats, flour, brown sugar, and butter until crumbly.
4. Sprinkle over apples and bake for 30-35 minutes until bubbly.

Enjoy these delicious treats!

Lemon Bars

Ingredients:

For the crust:
1 cup all-purpose flour
1/2 cup powdered sugar
1/2 cup butter, softened

For the filling:
1 cup granulated sugar
2 large eggs
1/4 cup fresh lemon juice
1 tsp lemon zest
1/4 cup all-purpose flour
1/2 tsp baking powder
Powdered sugar for dusting

Instructions:

1. Preheat oven to 350°F (175°C). Grease an 8x8-inch baking dish.
2. In a bowl, mix flour, powdered sugar, and butter until crumbly. Press into the bottom of the dish.
3. Bake for 15 minutes.
4. In another bowl, whisk together sugar, eggs, lemon juice, lemon zest, flour, and baking powder. Pour over the crust.
5. Bake for an additional 20-25 minutes until set. Let cool and dust with powdered sugar before slicing.

Sugar Cookies

Ingredients:
1 cup butter, softened
1 1/2 cups granulated sugar
1 large egg
1 tsp vanilla extract
3 cups all-purpose flour
1 tsp baking powder
1/2 tsp salt

Instructions:

1. Preheat oven to 350°F (175°C).
2. In a bowl, cream together butter and sugar. Beat in egg and vanilla.
3. In another bowl, combine flour, baking powder, and salt. Gradually add to the wet mixture.
4. Roll into balls, place on a baking sheet, and flatten slightly. Bake for 8-10 minutes until lightly golden.

Oatmeal Cookies

Ingredients:
1 cup butter, softened
1 cup brown sugar
1/2 cup granulated sugar
2 large eggs
1 tsp vanilla extract
1 1/2 cups all-purpose flour
1 tsp baking soda
1/2 tsp salt
3 cups rolled oats
1 cup raisins or chocolate chips (optional)

Instructions:

1. Preheat oven to 350°F (175°C).
2. In a bowl, cream together butter, brown sugar, and granulated sugar. Add eggs and vanilla; mix well.
3. In another bowl, whisk flour, baking soda, and salt. Gradually mix into the wet ingredients.
4. Stir in oats and raisins or chocolate chips if using. Drop spoonfuls onto a baking sheet and bake for 10-12 minutes.

Chocolate Mousse

Ingredients:
6 oz semi-sweet chocolate, chopped
3 tbsp butter
3 large eggs, separated
1/4 cup granulated sugar
1 cup heavy cream
1 tsp vanilla extract

Instructions:

1. Melt chocolate and butter in a bowl over simmering water; let cool slightly.
2. In a separate bowl, beat egg yolks with sugar until pale. Stir in melted chocolate and vanilla.
3. In another bowl, whip cream until soft peaks form, then fold into chocolate mixture.
4. Beat egg whites until stiff peaks form; gently fold into the mousse. Chill for at least 2 hours before serving.

Mini Fruit Tarts

Ingredients:
For the crust:
1 1/2 cups all-purpose flour
1/2 cup butter, softened
1/4 cup powdered sugar
1 egg yolk

For the filling:
1 cup pastry cream or vanilla pudding
Mixed fresh fruits (berries, kiwi, etc.)

Instructions:

1. Preheat oven to 350°F (175°C).
2. In a bowl, mix flour, butter, powdered sugar, and egg yolk until a dough forms. Press into mini tart pans.
3. Bake for 10-12 minutes until golden. Let cool.
4. Fill each tart with pastry cream and top with fresh fruits.

Snickerdoodles

Ingredients:
1 cup butter, softened
1 1/2 cups granulated sugar
2 large eggs
1 tsp vanilla extract
2 3/4 cups all-purpose flour
1 tsp cream of tartar
1/2 tsp baking soda
1/4 tsp salt
Cinnamon sugar for rolling

Instructions:

1. Preheat oven to 350°F (175°C).
2. In a bowl, cream together butter and sugar. Beat in eggs and vanilla.
3. In another bowl, mix flour, cream of tartar, baking soda, and salt. Gradually combine with wet ingredients.
4. Roll dough into balls, roll in cinnamon sugar, and place on a baking sheet. Bake for 8-10 minutes.

Muffins

Ingredients:
2 cups all-purpose flour
1/2 cup sugar
2 tsp baking powder
1/2 tsp baking soda
1/2 tsp salt
1 cup milk
1/3 cup vegetable oil
1 large egg
1 cup blueberries or chocolate chips (optional)

Instructions:

1. Preheat oven to 375°F (190°C). Line a muffin tin with liners.
2. In a bowl, combine flour, sugar, baking powder, baking soda, and salt.
3. In another bowl, mix milk, oil, and egg. Combine wet and dry ingredients until just mixed. Fold in blueberries or chocolate chips if using.
4. Fill muffin cups 2/3 full and bake for 15-20 minutes until a toothpick comes out clean.

Pudding Cups

Ingredients:
2 cups milk
1/2 cup granulated sugar
1/4 cup cornstarch
1/4 tsp salt
2 tsp vanilla extract
Whipped cream and chocolate shavings for topping

Instructions:

1. In a saucepan, whisk together sugar, cornstarch, and salt. Gradually add milk and cook over medium heat, stirring until thickened.
2. Remove from heat and stir in vanilla.
3. Pour into cups and chill until set. Top with whipped cream and chocolate shavings before serving.

Enjoy these delightful treats!

Cookie Dough Truffles

Ingredients:
1/2 cup unsalted butter, softened
1 cup brown sugar
1 tsp vanilla extract
1 cup all-purpose flour
1/2 tsp salt
1/2 cup mini chocolate chips
1 cup chocolate chips (for coating)

Instructions:

1. In a bowl, cream together butter and brown sugar. Add vanilla and mix well.
2. Stir in flour and salt, then fold in mini chocolate chips.
3. Roll mixture into small balls and place on a baking sheet. Freeze for about 30 minutes.
4. Melt chocolate chips in a microwave or double boiler. Dip each frozen ball in melted chocolate and place on parchment paper to set.

Chocolate-Covered Pretzels

Ingredients:
2 cups pretzels (regular or mini)
1 cup chocolate chips (milk, dark, or white)
Sprinkles or crushed nuts (optional)

Instructions:

1. Melt chocolate chips in a microwave-safe bowl, stirring every 30 seconds until smooth.
2. Dip pretzels into melted chocolate, ensuring they are well-coated.
3. Place on parchment paper and sprinkle with toppings if desired.
4. Let chocolate set at room temperature or refrigerate until firm.

Granola Bars

Ingredients:
2 cups rolled oats
1/2 cup honey or maple syrup
1/2 cup nut butter (peanut or almond)
1/2 cup nuts and seeds (almonds, pumpkin seeds)
1/2 cup dried fruits (raisins, cranberries)
1 tsp vanilla extract

Instructions:

1. Preheat oven to 350°F (175°C) and line a baking dish with parchment paper.
2. In a large bowl, mix oats, nuts, seeds, and dried fruits.
3. In a small saucepan, heat honey and nut butter until melted. Stir in vanilla.
4. Pour wet mixture over dry ingredients and mix until well combined.
5. Press mixture into the prepared baking dish and bake for 20-25 minutes. Let cool before cutting into bars.

Fruit Salad

Ingredients:
2 cups strawberries, hulled and sliced
2 cups blueberries
2 cups kiwi, peeled and sliced
2 cups pineapple, diced
Juice of 1 lime
Honey (optional)

Instructions:

1. In a large bowl, combine all fruits.
2. Drizzle with lime juice and honey, if using.
3. Toss gently to combine and serve immediately or chill before serving.

Cake Pops

Ingredients:
1 cake (any flavor, baked and cooled)
1/2 cup frosting (store-bought or homemade)
1 cup chocolate or candy melts (for coating)
Lollipop sticks

Instructions:

1. Crumble the cooled cake into a large bowl and mix in frosting until combined.
2. Roll mixture into small balls and place on a baking sheet. Freeze for 30 minutes.
3. Melt chocolate or candy melts. Dip the end of each lollipop stick into chocolate, then insert into each ball.
4. Dip each cake pop into melted chocolate and let set on parchment paper.

S'mores

Ingredients:
Graham crackers
Chocolate bars
Marshmallows

Instructions:

1. Preheat oven to 400°F (200°C) or prepare a campfire.
2. On a baking sheet, layer half of the graham crackers with chocolate squares and top with marshmallows.
3. Bake for 5-7 minutes until marshmallows are toasted.
4. Remove from oven and top with remaining graham crackers to create sandwiches.

Shortbread Cookies

Ingredients:
1 cup unsalted butter, softened
1/2 cup powdered sugar
2 cups all-purpose flour
1/4 tsp salt

Instructions:

1. Preheat oven to 325°F (165°C).
2. In a bowl, cream together butter and powdered sugar until light and fluffy.
3. Gradually mix in flour and salt until combined.
4. Roll dough into balls or press into a tart pan. Bake for 15-20 minutes until lightly golden.

Eclairs

Ingredients:
For the choux pastry:
1 cup water
1/2 cup unsalted butter
1 cup all-purpose flour
4 large eggs

For the filling:
1 cup heavy cream
1/4 cup powdered sugar
1 tsp vanilla extract

For the chocolate glaze:
1 cup chocolate chips
1/2 cup heavy cream

Instructions:

1. Preheat oven to 400°F (200°C).
2. In a saucepan, bring water and butter to a boil. Stir in flour until combined and cook for 1-2 minutes.
3. Remove from heat and add eggs one at a time, mixing until smooth.
4. Pipe the dough onto a baking sheet into 4-inch lines. Bake for 20-25 minutes until puffed and golden.
5. For the filling, whip cream with powdered sugar and vanilla until stiff peaks form. Fill cooled eclairs.
6. For the glaze, heat cream and pour over chocolate chips; stir until smooth. Dip tops of eclairs into glaze.

Enjoy these delicious treats!

Fudge

Ingredients:
2 cups semi-sweet chocolate chips
1 cup sweetened condensed milk
1/4 cup butter
1 tsp vanilla extract
Pinch of salt

Instructions:

1. Line an 8x8-inch baking dish with parchment paper.
2. In a saucepan, melt chocolate chips, condensed milk, butter, and salt over low heat, stirring until smooth.
3. Remove from heat and stir in vanilla.
4. Pour into the prepared dish and spread evenly. Refrigerate until set, then cut into squares.

Blondies

Ingredients:
1/2 cup butter, melted
1 cup brown sugar
1/2 cup granulated sugar
1 large egg
1 tsp vanilla extract
1 1/2 cups all-purpose flour
1/2 tsp baking powder
1/4 tsp salt
1 cup chocolate chips (optional)

Instructions:

1. Preheat oven to 350°F (175°C) and grease an 8x8-inch baking pan.
2. In a bowl, mix melted butter, brown sugar, and granulated sugar until combined.
3. Stir in egg and vanilla. Add flour, baking powder, and salt; mix until just combined.
4. Fold in chocolate chips if using. Pour batter into the prepared pan and bake for 20-25 minutes.

Chocolate Bark

Ingredients:
2 cups chocolate chips (milk, dark, or white)
1 cup mixed nuts, dried fruits, or candies (optional)

Instructions:

1. Melt chocolate chips in a microwave-safe bowl, stirring every 30 seconds until smooth.
2. Spread melted chocolate onto a parchment-lined baking sheet.
3. Sprinkle nuts, dried fruits, or candies on top and gently press them into the chocolate.
4. Refrigerate until set, then break into pieces.

Pancakes with Syrup

Ingredients:
1 cup all-purpose flour
2 tbsp sugar
1 tsp baking powder
1/2 tsp baking soda
1/4 tsp salt
1 cup milk
1 large egg
2 tbsp melted butter
Maple syrup for serving

Instructions:

1. In a bowl, whisk together flour, sugar, baking powder, baking soda, and salt.
2. In another bowl, mix milk, egg, and melted butter. Combine wet and dry ingredients until just mixed.
3. Heat a skillet over medium heat and pour batter to form pancakes. Cook until bubbles form, then flip and cook until golden.
4. Serve warm with maple syrup.

Strawberry Shortcake

Ingredients:
For the biscuits:
2 cups all-purpose flour
1/4 cup sugar
1 tbsp baking powder
1/2 tsp salt
1/2 cup cold butter, cubed
3/4 cup milk

For the filling:
4 cups strawberries, hulled and sliced
1/4 cup sugar
1 cup whipped cream

Instructions:

1. Preheat oven to 425°F (220°C).
2. In a bowl, mix flour, sugar, baking powder, and salt. Cut in butter until mixture resembles coarse crumbs.
3. Stir in milk until just combined. Drop dough onto a baking sheet and bake for 12-15 minutes.
4. In a bowl, toss strawberries with sugar and let sit for 15 minutes.
5. Split biscuits in half, layer with strawberries and whipped cream, then top with the other half.

Biscotti

Ingredients:
2 cups all-purpose flour
1 cup sugar
1/2 tsp baking powder
1/4 tsp salt
2 large eggs
1 tsp vanilla extract
1 cup chopped nuts (almonds, pistachios)

Instructions:

1. Preheat oven to 350°F (175°C) and line a baking sheet with parchment paper.
2. In a bowl, mix flour, sugar, baking powder, and salt. In another bowl, whisk eggs and vanilla.
3. Combine wet and dry ingredients; fold in nuts.
4. Shape dough into a log and bake for 25 minutes. Let cool, slice into pieces, and bake again for 10-15 minutes until crisp.

Tiramisu

Ingredients:
1 cup brewed coffee, cooled
1/4 cup coffee liqueur (optional)
3 large eggs, separated
1/2 cup sugar
8 oz mascarpone cheese
1 cup heavy cream
24 ladyfinger cookies
Cocoa powder for dusting

Instructions:

1. In a bowl, combine coffee and liqueur.
2. In another bowl, beat egg yolks with sugar until pale and creamy. Mix in mascarpone until smooth.
3. In a separate bowl, whip cream to soft peaks, then fold into mascarpone mixture.
4. Dip ladyfingers into coffee mixture and layer them in a dish. Spread half the mascarpone mixture on top. Repeat layers.
5. Refrigerate for at least 4 hours. Dust with cocoa powder before serving.

Chocolate Dipped Strawberries

Ingredients:
1 lb fresh strawberries, washed and dried
1 cup semi-sweet chocolate chips
1 tbsp coconut oil (optional)

Instructions:

1. Melt chocolate chips and coconut oil in a microwave-safe bowl, stirring every 30 seconds until smooth.
2. Dip each strawberry into the melted chocolate, allowing excess to drip off.
3. Place on parchment paper and refrigerate until chocolate is set.

Enjoy these delicious desserts!

Meringue Cookies

Ingredients:
3 large egg whites
1/4 tsp cream of tartar
3/4 cup granulated sugar
1 tsp vanilla extract

Instructions:

1. Preheat oven to 225°F (110°C) and line a baking sheet with parchment paper.
2. In a clean, dry bowl, beat egg whites and cream of tartar until soft peaks form.
3. Gradually add sugar, continuing to beat until stiff peaks form. Mix in vanilla.
4. Spoon or pipe meringue onto the prepared baking sheet.
5. Bake for 1 to 1.5 hours until dry and crisp. Turn off the oven and let meringues cool inside.

Energy Bites

Ingredients:
1 cup rolled oats
1/2 cup peanut butter (or almond butter)
1/3 cup honey
1/2 cup chocolate chips
1/4 cup ground flaxseed
1/4 cup chopped nuts or seeds

Instructions:

1. In a bowl, combine all ingredients and mix until well combined.
2. Roll the mixture into bite-sized balls and place on a baking sheet.
3. Refrigerate for at least 30 minutes to set. Store in an airtight container in the fridge.

Chocolate Lava Cake

Ingredients:
1/2 cup unsalted butter
1 cup semi-sweet chocolate chips
2 large eggs
2 large egg yolks
1/4 cup granulated sugar
2 tbsp all-purpose flour
1/4 tsp salt

Instructions:

1. Preheat oven to 425°F (220°C). Grease four ramekins.
2. Melt butter and chocolate chips together in a microwave-safe bowl.
3. In another bowl, whisk eggs, egg yolks, and sugar until thick.
4. Stir in chocolate mixture, then fold in flour and salt.
5. Divide batter among ramekins and bake for 12-14 minutes. Let cool for 1 minute, then invert onto plates.

Crepes

Ingredients:
1 cup all-purpose flour
2 large eggs
1 1/2 cups milk
2 tbsp melted butter
1/4 tsp salt
Butter or oil for cooking

Instructions:

1. In a bowl, whisk flour, eggs, milk, melted butter, and salt until smooth.
2. Heat a non-stick skillet over medium heat and lightly grease with butter or oil.
3. Pour about 1/4 cup batter into the skillet, swirling to coat the bottom.
4. Cook for 1-2 minutes until lightly browned, then flip and cook for another minute. Repeat with remaining batter.
5. Fill with your choice of sweet or savory fillings.

Coconut Macaroons

Ingredients:
2 2/3 cups shredded coconut
1/2 cup sweetened condensed milk
1 tsp vanilla extract
1/4 tsp salt
4 large egg whites

Instructions:

1. Preheat oven to 325°F (165°C) and line a baking sheet with parchment paper.
2. In a bowl, mix coconut, condensed milk, vanilla, and salt.
3. In another bowl, beat egg whites until stiff peaks form, then gently fold into the coconut mixture.
4. Drop spoonfuls onto the baking sheet and bake for 20-25 minutes until golden brown.

Rice Pudding

Ingredients:
1 cup cooked rice
2 cups milk
1/4 cup sugar
1/2 tsp vanilla extract
1/4 tsp cinnamon
1/4 cup raisins (optional)

Instructions:

1. In a saucepan, combine cooked rice, milk, sugar, and cinnamon.
2. Cook over medium heat, stirring frequently, until the mixture thickens (about 15-20 minutes).
3. Stir in vanilla and raisins, if using. Serve warm or chilled.

Cinnamon Rolls

Ingredients:
For the dough:
2 1/4 tsp active dry yeast
3/4 cup milk, warmed
1/4 cup sugar
1/4 cup butter, melted
1/2 tsp salt
1 large egg
2 1/4 cups all-purpose flour

For the filling:
1/4 cup butter, softened
1/2 cup brown sugar
1 tbsp cinnamon

For the icing:
1 cup powdered sugar
2 tbsp milk
1/2 tsp vanilla extract

Instructions:

1. In a bowl, combine yeast and warm milk; let sit for 5 minutes.
2. Add sugar, melted butter, salt, egg, and flour; mix until a dough forms. Knead until smooth.
3. Let rise for 1 hour.
4. Roll out dough, spread with softened butter, and sprinkle with brown sugar and cinnamon. Roll up tightly and slice into rolls.
5. Place in a greased baking dish and let rise for 30 minutes. Preheat oven to 375°F (190°C) and bake for 20-25 minutes.
6. Mix icing ingredients and drizzle over warm rolls.

Milkshakes

Ingredients:
2 cups vanilla ice cream
1 cup milk
1 tsp vanilla extract (optional)
Toppings: whipped cream, chocolate syrup, sprinkles

Instructions:

1. In a blender, combine ice cream, milk, and vanilla extract. Blend until smooth.
2. Adjust consistency by adding more milk if desired.
3. Pour into glasses and top with whipped cream and any desired toppings.

Enjoy these delightful treats!

Fruit Smoothies

Ingredients:
1 cup frozen fruit (e.g., berries, mango)
1 banana
1 cup yogurt or milk (dairy or non-dairy)
1 tbsp honey or maple syrup (optional)
1 tbsp chia seeds (optional)

Instructions:

1. In a blender, combine frozen fruit, banana, yogurt or milk, honey, and chia seeds.
2. Blend until smooth and creamy.
3. Pour into glasses and serve immediately.

Chocolate Banana Pops

Ingredients:
2 ripe bananas
1 cup semi-sweet chocolate chips
1 tbsp coconut oil (optional)
Sprinkles or crushed nuts (optional)

Instructions:

1. Cut bananas in half and insert sticks into each piece.
2. Melt chocolate chips and coconut oil in a microwave-safe bowl, stirring until smooth.
3. Dip each banana half into the melted chocolate, allowing excess to drip off.
4. Roll in sprinkles or crushed nuts if desired.
5. Place on a parchment-lined baking sheet and freeze until firm.

Apple Pie

Ingredients:
For the crust:
2 1/2 cups all-purpose flour
1 tsp salt
1 tsp sugar
1 cup unsalted butter, chilled and cubed
6-8 tbsp ice water

For the filling:
6 cups sliced apples (e.g., Granny Smith, Honeycrisp)
3/4 cup sugar
2 tbsp flour
1 tsp cinnamon
1 tbsp lemon juice

Instructions:

1. Preheat oven to 425°F (220°C).
2. In a bowl, combine flour, salt, and sugar. Cut in butter until the mixture resembles coarse crumbs.
3. Gradually add ice water until dough forms. Divide in half, shape into discs, and refrigerate for 30 minutes.
4. Roll out one dough disc and place in a pie dish. Mix filling ingredients and pour into the crust.
5. Roll out the second dough disc, place over filling, and seal edges. Cut slits in the top for steam to escape.
6. Bake for 45-50 minutes until apples are tender and crust is golden.

Gingerbread Cookies

Ingredients:
3 1/4 cups all-purpose flour
1 tsp baking soda
1 tbsp ground ginger
1 tbsp ground cinnamon
1/2 tsp ground cloves
1/2 tsp salt
3/4 cup unsalted butter, softened
1 cup brown sugar
1/2 cup molasses
1 large egg

Instructions:

1. Preheat oven to 350°F (175°C).
2. In a bowl, whisk flour, baking soda, ginger, cinnamon, cloves, and salt.
3. In another bowl, cream butter and brown sugar. Add molasses and egg, mixing until smooth.
4. Gradually add dry ingredients, mixing until well combined.
5. Roll out dough and cut into shapes. Bake for 8-10 minutes. Let cool before decorating.

Cookie Cups

Ingredients:
1 cup unsalted butter, softened
1 cup granulated sugar
1 cup brown sugar
2 large eggs
2 tsp vanilla extract
3 cups all-purpose flour
1 tsp baking soda
1/2 tsp salt

Instructions:

1. Preheat oven to 350°F (175°C).
2. In a bowl, cream together butter, granulated sugar, and brown sugar. Add eggs and vanilla, mixing well.
3. In another bowl, whisk flour, baking soda, and salt. Gradually add to the wet mixture.
4. Grease a muffin tin and scoop dough into each cup, pressing down to form a cup shape.
5. Bake for 10-12 minutes until golden. Let cool before filling with your favorite frosting or ganache.

Pumpkin Spice Muffins

Ingredients:
1 1/2 cups all-purpose flour
1 cup sugar
1 tsp baking powder
1/2 tsp baking soda
1/2 tsp salt
1 tsp cinnamon
1/2 tsp nutmeg
1/2 tsp ginger
1 cup pumpkin puree
1/2 cup vegetable oil
2 large eggs
1 tsp vanilla extract

Instructions:

1. Preheat oven to 350°F (175°C) and line a muffin tin with paper liners.
2. In a bowl, mix flour, sugar, baking powder, baking soda, salt, cinnamon, nutmeg, and ginger.
3. In another bowl, whisk pumpkin, oil, eggs, and vanilla. Combine wet and dry ingredients until just mixed.
4. Fill muffin cups about 2/3 full and bake for 20-25 minutes. Let cool before serving.

Sweet Potato Pie

Ingredients:
1 pie crust (store-bought or homemade)
2 cups mashed sweet potatoes
3/4 cup brown sugar
1/2 cup milk
2 large eggs
1 tsp vanilla extract
1 tsp cinnamon
1/2 tsp nutmeg
1/4 tsp salt

Instructions:

1. Preheat oven to 350°F (175°C).
2. In a bowl, mix mashed sweet potatoes, brown sugar, milk, eggs, vanilla, cinnamon, nutmeg, and salt until smooth.
3. Pour filling into the pie crust and smooth the top.
4. Bake for 45-50 minutes until set. Let cool before serving.

Churros

Ingredients:
1 cup water
1/2 cup unsalted butter
1/4 tsp salt
1 cup all-purpose flour
2 large eggs
1 tsp vanilla extract
1/2 cup sugar (for coating)
1 tbsp cinnamon (for coating)
Oil for frying

Instructions:

1. In a saucepan, bring water, butter, and salt to a boil. Remove from heat and stir in flour until a dough forms.
2. Allow to cool slightly, then mix in eggs and vanilla until smooth.
3. Heat oil in a deep pan to 375°F (190°C). Pipe dough into the hot oil, cutting to your desired length.
4. Fry until golden brown, then drain on paper towels. Mix sugar and cinnamon, and coat the churros while warm.

Enjoy these delightful treats!

Ice Cream Sundaes

Ingredients:

- 2 cups ice cream (any flavor)
- 1/2 cup chocolate or caramel sauce
- Whipped cream
- Chopped nuts (e.g., pecans, walnuts)
- Maraschino cherries
- Optional toppings: sprinkles, fresh fruit, crushed cookies

Instructions:

1. Scoop the ice cream into bowls or dessert glasses.
2. Drizzle chocolate or caramel sauce over the ice cream.
3. Add a generous dollop of whipped cream on top.
4. Sprinkle with chopped nuts and any additional toppings you like.
5. Finish with a maraschino cherry on top. Serve immediately.

Pecan Pie

Ingredients:
For the crust:

- 1 1/4 cups all-purpose flour
- 1/4 tsp salt
- 1/2 cup unsalted butter, chilled and cubed
- 1/4 cup ice water

For the filling:

- 1 cup corn syrup
- 1 cup brown sugar
- 4 large eggs
- 2 tbsp unsalted butter, melted
- 1 tsp vanilla extract
- 1 1/2 cups pecans

Instructions:

1. Preheat the oven to 350°F (175°C).
2. **Make the crust:** In a bowl, mix flour and salt. Cut in butter until the mixture resembles coarse crumbs. Gradually add ice water until dough forms. Shape into a disc and refrigerate for 30 minutes.
3. Roll out the dough and fit it into a pie dish. Trim excess.
4. **Make the filling:** In a bowl, whisk together corn syrup, brown sugar, eggs, melted butter, and vanilla. Stir in pecans.
5. Pour filling into the prepared crust.
6. Bake for 50-60 minutes, or until the filling is set and the crust is golden.
7. Let cool before slicing. Enjoy!

Enjoy your treats!

www.ingramcontent.com/pod-product-compliance
Lightning Source LLC
LaVergne TN
LVHW061953070526
838199LV00060B/4095